Healthy HABITS™

Living a Heart-Healthy Life

Michael R. Wilson

rosen publishing's
rosen central®

New York

Published in 2011 by The Rosen Publishing Group, Inc.
29 East 21st Street, New York, NY 10010

Copyright © 2011 by The Rosen Publishing Group, Inc.

First Edition

Library of Congress Cataloging-in-Publication Data

Wilson, Michael R., 1967–
Living a heart-healthy life / Michael R. Wilson.—1st ed.
    p. cm.—(Healthy habits)
Includes bibliographical references and index.
ISBN 978-1-4358-9438-9 (library binding)
ISBN 978-1-4488-0608-9 (pbk)
ISBN 978-1-4488-0615-7 (6-pack)
1. Heart—Physiology—Juvenile literature. 2. Exercise—Juvenile literature. 3. Health—Juvenile literature. I. Title.
QP111.6.W55 2011
612.1'7—dc22

                                                                    2009047916

Manufactured in Malaysia

CPSIA Compliance Information: Batch #S10YA: For further information, contact Rosen Publishing, New York, New York, at 1-800-237-9932.

CONTENTS

Introduction

The heart is one of the most important organs in your body. When the heart is working well in a healthy person, you hardly know it's there. Muscular and about the size of a clenched fist, it acts like a pump, flexing and squeezing to push blood out of its chambers and through a network of vessels to your core, your limbs, and your brain. The heart of a sick person, like someone with heart disease, is a different story. A diseased heart can't do its job efficiently. A damaged heart can't pump like it's supposed to, so it has trouble sending blood to the places where blood is needed most. People with hearts that aren't healthy are like ticking time bombs. When the heart goes, it's serious trouble.

Keeping your heart healthy, then, is critical. Having a healthy heart is like having a clean, well-tuned engine in your car. It's reliable. It's unlikely to break down. So what is the key to maintaining a healthy heart? In short, it's developing healthy habits and making healthy choices. If you make the right decisions about diet, exercise, and lifestyle, your heart will likely stay healthy, and so will you.

Of course, maintaining a healthy heart is not always that simple. Some people are born with heart defects, and others develop heart diseases later in life that are unrelated to lifestyle decisions. Genetics can play a large role in who develops heart problems and who stays healthy. When it comes to heart health, there's a fair amount of luck involved.

Whether or not heart disease runs in your family, you should do your best to keep your heart in top shape. If you don't exercise, or

Running is a fun way to build muscle and stay fit. Plus, the cardiovascular exercise is great for your heart!

only exercise rarely, you can pick up the pace. If you tend to eat a lot of junk food, you can call it quits and make eating well a habit. You can do other things, too, as you'll soon see. Why not make the changes in your life that will make your heart healthier? They're easy. They can be fun. And best of all? You can start right now.

Maintaining a healthy heart involves a lifetime commitment. Develop good habits now, while you're young, and they'll stick with you for the rest of your life. Later, when you're old and it seems as if everyone around you is breaking down, you just might find that your heart is stronger than ever.

Chapter 1

Healthy Heart Basics

The healthy heart, found between the lungs near the center of the chest, is surrounded by a thin, protective layer of fat, but other than that it's mostly muscle. Its job is to pump your blood and to supply your entire body with the oxygen and nutrients you need to survive.

The healthy heart is divided into two major halves: right and left. The right heart, as it's known, pumps blood to the lungs. There, carbon dioxide, a waste product that results during metabolism (the process by which cells use oxygen to convert food to energy), is expelled. At the same time, the air the lungs take in replenishes the blood with oxygen. The left heart takes in that oxygen-rich blood, and with a well-timed contraction, sends it out again to the rest of the body.

Each side of the heart includes two chambers: each has one atrium and one ventricle. Atria, found on the top, are chambers where blood enters the heart. Ventricles, on the bottom, send blood away. There are valves between the chambers, nerves, and arteries, and veins are all over the place to keep the heart functioning. Some vessels are very small and supply the heart itself with nourishment. Others, like the pulmonary artery, the pulmonary vein, and the aorta, are huge. The aorta, which comes from the left ventricle, is the largest blood vessel in the body. It's the main line of passage for every drop of blood the heart pumps out.

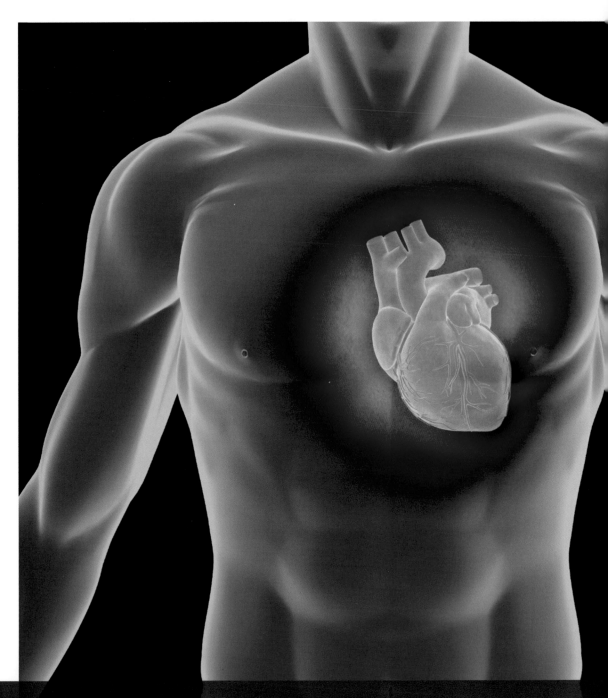

The heart is one of the most important organs you have. Its huge vessels and muscular, power-ful chambers pump and deliver blood to every cell in your body.

The healthy heart is warm, richly red, and pulsing. It works efficiently and smoothly. Its beats are strong and regular. It teems with electrical activity—the invisible, carefully coordinated signals between cells that determine when each chamber contracts. The healthy heart, were you to touch it, would feel vibrantly alive. And it is. The heart is your body's anchor. You can't live, let alone play, exercise, or enjoy life to the fullest, without it.

The Unhealthy Heart

The unhealthy heart is an entirely different story. In many cases, the unhealthy heart, at least at first glance, might look a lot like the healthy heart—big, vibrant, and alive with energy. A closer look, however, would likely reveal some differences.

You might find that certain arteries supplying the heart with blood have narrowed and even pinched off in places. You might see signs of disease and decay, like blotchy patches or dark spots. You might find that the muscle fibers have become tough and brittle. The heart's color might appear off, even pale.

Beyond its outward appearance, there's also function to consider. Plain and simple, the unhealthy heart isn't able to do the things it's supposed to do. If a coronary artery is clogged, that means the heart is not getting the oxygen and nutrients it

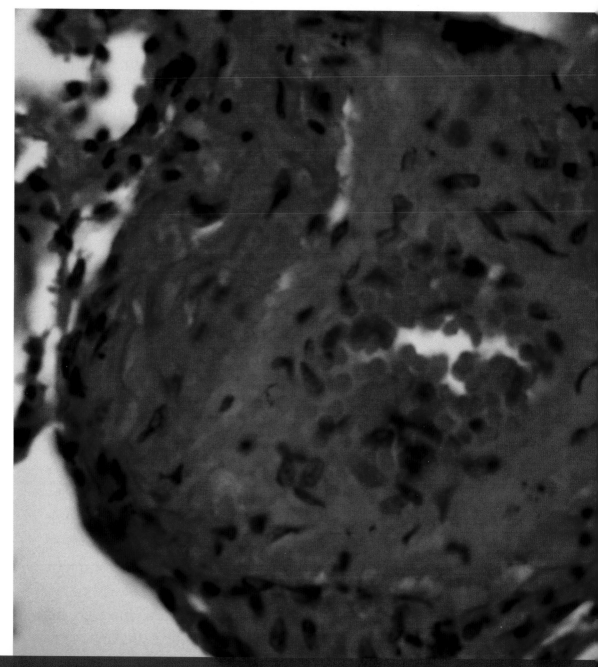

Modern imaging techniques allow doctors and researchers to see the heart in action and to diagnose disease. A damaged cardiovascular system might include a greatly thickened arteriole (small branch of an artery), like the one above.

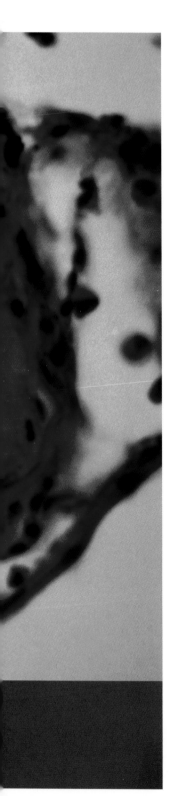

needs for nourishment. If a valve is leaking, then blood is not traveling in the direction it's meant to travel. If fibers are tight or brittle, then contractions can't take place efficiently and blood flow will be weak. For the rest of the body, of course, this is very bad news. A weak or inefficient heart means less blood for the places it's needed most—like the brain. When your heart doesn't work, the rest of your body can't work either.

The Big Killer: Heart Disease

According to the National Heart, Lung, and Blood Institute (NHLBI), the problem that most people have to watch out for is heart disease. Heart disease, also known as coronary artery disease, is the number one killer of both men and women in the United States. Heart disease is a condition in which arteries that deliver blood to the heart (the coronary arteries) build up plaque and become hard and narrow. The plaque, which is mainly excess fat and cholesterol, clings to the inner artery walls and blocks or limits the passage of blood. If the blockage becomes severe, the individual may suffer a heart attack. During a heart attack (also known as a myocardial infarction), the heart stops working properly because it is no longer getting the oxygen and nutrients it needs to function. Some of the heart tissue dies or becomes permanently damaged.

Anatomy of the Coronary Arteries with Potential Blockages

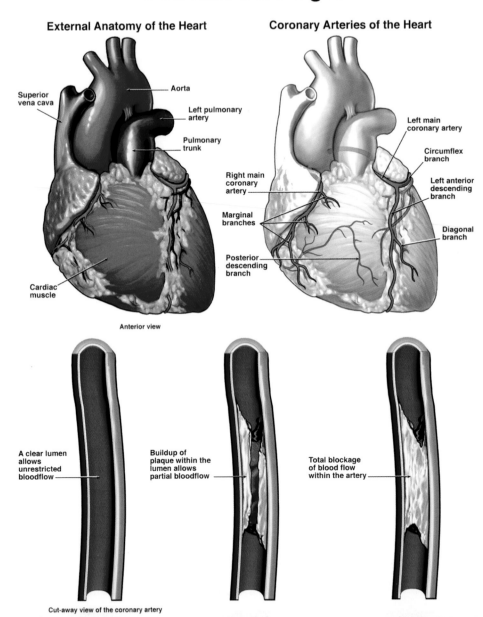

External Anatomy of the Heart

Superior vena cava

Aorta

Left pulmonary artery

Pulmonary trunk

Cardiac muscle

Anterior view

Coronary Arteries of the Heart

Left main coronary artery

Circumflex branch

Left anterior descending branch

Right main coronary artery

Marginal branches

Posterior descending branch

Diagonal branch

A clear lumen allows unrestricted bloodflow

Buildup of plaque within the lumen allows partial bloodflow

Total blockage of blood flow within the artery

Cut-away view of the coronary artery

The coronary arteries nourish the heart with oxygen-rich blood. If a person's heart loses its oxygen supply due to narrowed or blocked coronary arteries, the person may have a heart attack.

Heart disease affects people of all ages, even some teenagers. Most teens with heart disease have congenital forms of the condition. They were born with a heart problem. You may have heard about young athletes dying on the basketball court or football field in the middle of a game. Sudden cardiac death, as this is known, is usually due to a congenital condition called genetic hypertrophic obstructive cardiomyopathy. Simply put, it's a thickening of the cardiac septum, the wall that divides the left side of the heart from the right. Some people may have been born with especially narrow blood vessels, extra holes in their cardiac septum, or genetic diseases involving poor cholesterol or lipid metabolism. (In this last example, patients are unable to break down these products in the bloodstream. The result, in rare cases, can be coronary artery blockage—a heart attack.)

Most victims of heart disease fall into another category altogether. These people are typically older (over age forty) and develop the condition over time because of poor lifestyle choices. Heart disease occurs most often among women over age forty-five and men over age fifty-five. About five hundred thousand Americans—half men, half women—die of heart disease every year. Many of those who die from heart disease show no prior symptoms of a heart condition.

Other Heart-Related Diseases

The heart, and more generally, the cardiovascular system, is susceptible to other problems as well. The cardiovascular system includes the heart and the blood vessels that supply the body with blood. Diseases and conditions that affect the cardiovascular system include stroke, high blood pressure (hypertension), and rheumatic heart disease. A stroke occurs when too little blood

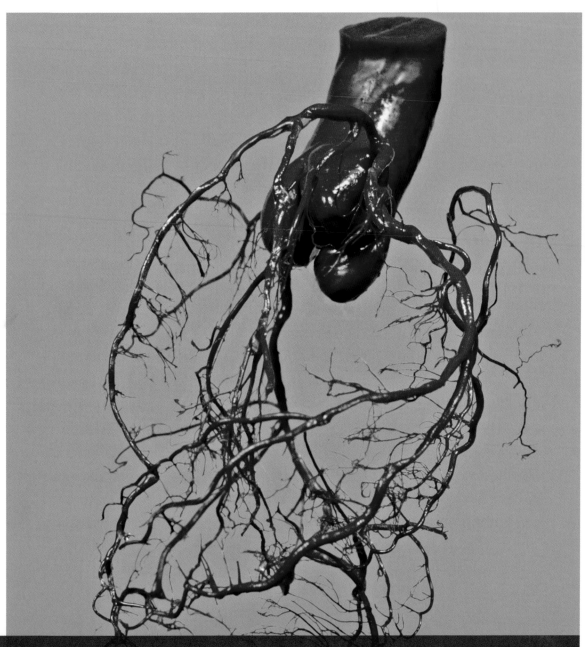

Atherosclerosis is the narrowing and hardening of the arteries due to a buildup of plaque on the artery walls. This resin cast shows what the coronary arteries and heart look like in a patient with the disease.

reaches the brain due to a blood clot within the brain's important blood vessels. Rheumatic heart disease occurs when the heart valves or muscles are damaged following rheumatic fever, a rare complication that results from untreated strep throat. Blood pressure is a measure of the force that blood exerts on the walls of blood vessels. High blood pressure is a problem because it is the primary cause of heart disease.

Risk Factors for Heart Disease

Certain habits, conditions, and circumstances can increase the likelihood that an individual will have health problems. Doctors call these conditions risk factors, and they make a point of looking for them during health exams. The major risk factors for heart problems are well known. Here's a rundown. We'll talk about reducing each risk later.

The primary risk factor for heart disease is high blood pressure. Also known as hypertension, high blood pressure is a problem in at least sixty-five million adults in the United States. Every year, more and more people, even some teenagers, develop high blood pressure.

Another major risk factor for heart disease is smoking. People who smoke cigarettes are six times more likely to have a heart attack than nonsmokers. In addition, those exposed to secondhand smoke on a regular basis have a 60 percent increased chance that they will develop heart disease.

A third risk factor is high cholesterol. While the body needs cholesterol to function, it makes all the cholesterol it needs on its own. People develop high cholesterol if they take in too much cholesterol through the diet or if they are predisposed to creating more cholesterol than the body needs. Extra cholesterol in the bloodstream can result in plaque buildup along the walls of arteries, leading to restrictions that prevent blood from flowing to the heart.

Another risk factor is being overweight. Almost two-thirds of Americans are considered overweight or obese. Among those ages six through nineteen, nearly 20 percent are overweight. Teenagers who are overweight are much more likely to be overweight as adults and are therefore much more likely to develop heart disease.

The last four major risk factors are physical inactivity (which is closely related to being overweight), diabetes (which is also common in overweight individuals), advanced age, and having a family history of heart disease. Advanced age is a risk factor because most of those who develop heart problems are older. A family history of heart disease can be a problem because sometimes heart conditions are

Choosing not to smoke is one of the best things you can do for your health. Cigarette smoke causes heart disease and other potentially fatal conditions, including lung cancer.

genetic. If you are predisposed to a heart condition because of your genes, you must be especially cautious about living your life in a way that maintains good health.

Before you write off risk factors, consider these statistics: Two-thirds of teenagers have at least one risk factor for heart disease. Most of those teens are either obese or have a family history of heart disease. Almost everyone who dies from heart disease has one or more of these risk factors. Those with more than one risk factor are at very high risk of developing heart disease. Risk factors are serious indicators of who will and who will not develop heart problems. Reduce or eliminate your risk factors, and you'll definitely increase your chances for remaining healthy.

Ten Great Questions
to Ask a Doctor

1. What is my risk for heart disease?

2. What is my blood pressure? What does it mean for me, and what do I need to do about it?

3. What are my cholesterol numbers? What do they mean for me, and what do I need to do about them?

4. What are my body mass index (BMI) and my waist measurement? Do they indicate that I need to lose weight for my health?

5. What is my blood sugar level? Does it mean I'm at risk for diabetes?

6. What other screening tests for heart disease do I need? How often should I return for checkups for my heart health?

7. For smokers: What can you do to help me quit smoking?

8. How much physical activity do I need to help protect my heart? What kinds of activities are helpful?

9. What is a heart-healthy eating plan for me? Should I see a registered dietitian or qualified nutritionist to learn more about healthy eating?

10. How can I tell if I'm having a heart attack?

Source: National Heart, Lung, and Blood Institute, National Institutes of Health (http://www.nhlbi.nih.gov/educational/hearttruth/lower-risk/ask-doctor.htm)

Chapter 2

Changing Your Diet

The NHLBI has determined that there are four specific habits that all people should follow if they wish to maintain a healthy heart. These habits, which are called the "Big Four," include eating a healthy diet, getting regular physical activity, maintaining a healthy weight, and not smoking.

If you think about it, diet, physical activity, and healthy weight are all related. After all, if you eat well and get lots of exercise, your weight will probably trend toward a healthy number. Not smoking, on the other hand, stands on its own. Don't smoke and you'll significantly reduce your chances of developing all kinds of health problems, from heart disease to cancer. Smoking is not a healthy habit.

In this chapter, we'll talk about diet. In the next, we'll cover exercise. Finally, in the last chapter, we'll talk about finding balance in your life. A balanced lifestyle recognizes the need for variation, stimulation, concentration, and body- and mind-friendly activities. We'll give tips for putting everything together so that healthy living feels easy.

What to Eat

We all have to eat to survive. And let's face it, eating is one of the greatest pleasures in life. There's nothing like a good meal. Here's

Healthy eating is one of the keys to a healthy heart. A diet full of fresh vegetables picked straight from the garden or purchased from a local farmer's market is one simple and delicious way to stay healthy.

the thing about food, though: there are good foods, and there are bad foods. Certain foods are good for your body and good for your heart. Other foods are bad for your body and bad for your heart. Eat the good foods and keep the bad to a minimum, and your heart will thank you. Eat nothing but bad foods, and you just might pay the price—with your health.

Some people eat horribly all their lives and still manage to live well into old age. They're lucky. Most of those who neglect to eat a healthy diet show it, especially in their weight.

The American Heart Association (AHA)—the biggest, most author-itative group in the United States devoted to heart health—says the

Sure, it takes time to prepare vegetables for eating. But the wait is worth it, and your heart will thank you.

artery-clogging process that leads to heart damage often begins when people are young. It's very important to think about heart health now, while you're still young, and not to wait until you're older when it may be too late.

The ideal heart-friendly diet, says the AHA, relies primarily on fruits and vegetables, whole grains, low-fat dairy products, beans, fish, and lean meat. It also avoids saturated and trans fats, cholesterol, and products with added sugar and salt. It sounds a bit complicated, but you can do it if you follow a few basic rules: Say "no" to fast food; eat fresh, whole, and unprocessed foods; read labels; watch what you drink; and cook, cook, cook.

Say "No" to Fast Food

In 2005, a study by the Cardiovascular Research and Education Foundation in Wausau, Wisconsin, showed that children who eat out frequently are more likely to develop cardiovascular disease than those who eat most of their meals at home. The researchers used diet and exercise surveys completed by more than six hundred children from the second, fifth, eighth, and eleventh grades. The children's average age was thirteen.

"We are seeing younger and younger patients with more aggressive cardiovascular disease, and we realized we needed to take a closer look at our young people to see when risk factors emerge and why," said the study's lead author, Karen Olson, a registered nurse. "We're concerned because we know that children who have cardiovascular risks grow up to be adults who have these risks."

After the surveys were completed, the researchers used a number of health tests to compare those who said they ate out four or more times per week (29 percent of the children) with those who ate out fewer than four times per week. The children who ate out the most exhibited a number of characteristics that put them at greater risk of developing cardiovascular disease later in life, including:

- Higher blood pressure.
- Lower levels of high-density lipoprotein (HDL—the good cholesterol).
- More low-density lipoprotein (LDL) particles. These are small and dense and therefore more likely to cause athero-sclerosis (plaque along arterial walls).
- Early signs of development of type 2 diabetes.
- A tendency to consume higher levels of starch, sugar, sodium, fat, and cholesterol.

The bottom line is you should avoid fast food as much as possible. Simply put, it's bad for you. It's especially bad for your heart.

Eat Fresh, Whole, and Minimally Processed Foods

Hand in hand with avoiding fast food is eating foods that are fresh, whole, and minimally processed. Fresh food is better for you. It hasn't been altered, added to, or blended with fats and sugars. It comes directly from the source—the tree, the ground, the sea, or the plant. It's full of vitamins and minerals. All of these things are good for your heart.

So how do you get your hands on fresh food? First of all, say good-bye to packaging. Unless it's fresh meat or fish, if it's in a package, it's probably been there too long to be considered truly fresh. A great way to find fresh fruits and vegetables is by shopping at your local farmer's market. If there's no farmer's market, try your grocery store, sticking to the "outside" aisles of the store—the displays along the walls that usually hold all the healthiest options. Do you know the best way to get fresh fruit and vegetables? Start your own garden.

Farmer's markets are great places to socialize, take in some fresh air, and, of course, buy vegetables. Go to your local market, and you'll probably find all sorts of exciting veggies you never knew existed.

Whole foods include fresh fruits and vegetables, but they also include foods like grains, rice, and beans—bulk items that haven't been altered since they've been harvested. Whole foods include cheese, butter, and milk, as well as meat and fish.

Minimally processed foods include certain whole-grain breads and crackers and natural nut butters. They've been ground up and, perhaps, baked, but they haven't been doused with additives like sugar, salt, or artificial chemicals designed to lengthen shelf life.

Read Labels

If most of your diet comes from fresh and whole foods, you won't be doing a lot of label reading because there won't be much packaging. Still, it's impossible to avoid packaging all the time, so when your meal does come in a package, take a minute to read the label. Look for—and avoid—simple sugars, salts (sodium), excess fat, and anything that isn't immediately understandable. Chemicals are often added to products to improve shelf life. They make it feasible to ship an item across the country and store it for months or even years. If a food product has more than five to seven ingredients or looks like it could survive a tsunami and not spoil, then it's probably best to leave it where you found it.

Another important part of the label is the information you'll find on the product's cholesterol, calorie, and fat content. Cholesterol—which causes clogged arteries—is a big problem for the heart. Choose foods that are low in cholesterol. Foods with lots of calories can be exactly what you need—if you're truly hungry. If, however, you eat high-calorie and high-fat foods all the time and don't get the exercise you need to burn off the extra fuel, you'll probably gain weight. And weight gain is a prime problem for the heart.

About Calories

The word "calorie" is short for "kilocalorie." It comes from the Latin *calor*, which means "heat." The term refers to the amount of energy contained in fats, carbohydrates, and proteins—three nutrients commonly found in food. Higher-calorie foods hold greater amounts of energy—energy available to fuel the human body for a healthy and active life.

How many calories a particular food contains depends on what's in it. Fats, for example, contain nine calories per gram, while proteins and carbohydrates contain four calories per gram. You can check food labels to determine just how many calories you are taking in.

How many calories your body needs to function on a daily basis depends on a number of factors, including your age, size, and physical condition. The number also depends on your level of activity: the more active you are, the more calories you need to keep moving.

Consume more calories than you burn, and the excess energy will be stored as fat. Consume fewer calories than your body requires, and you'll lack the energy you need to be physically active. Consume just the right amount, and your body, including your heart, will function at its best.

It's all right to indulge once in a while, but make it the exception to the rule. Gain too much weight, and you'll put yourself at risk for heart disease.

Watch What You Drink

You can look at soft drinks like you look at fast food. Most bottled drinks, especially soda, are full of sugar that does nothing but put on extra pounds that may ultimately strain your heart. Experts say such sugary drinks are full of empty calories. That is, the calories they contain won't give you the nutritional boost you need for the long haul.

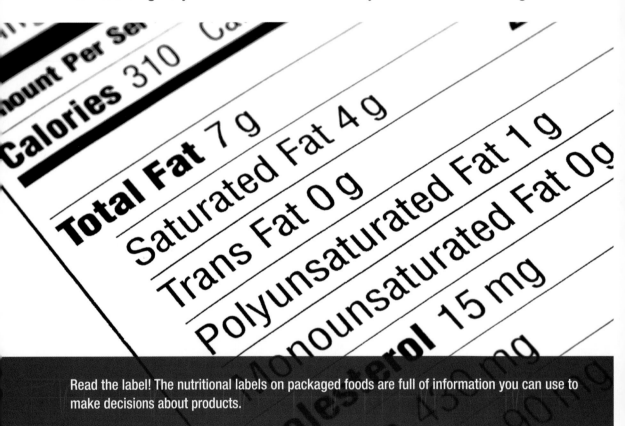

Read the label! The nutritional labels on packaged foods are full of information you can use to make decisions about products.

Avoiding soda is one really easy way to keep your weight in a healthy range. Study after study has shown that soda is a prime culprit in contributing to people becoming overweight or obese. To take care of your heart, drink plain water instead. Also be wary of drinks

It is important to stay hydrated in the heat of competition. Plain water is best, but an occasional sports drink can replenish the calories an athlete burns during strenuous exercise.

marketed as "vitamin waters," and limit your juice consumption. Such drinks, as well as energy drinks, are often full of sugar!

Cook, Cook, Cook

The more you (or your family) cook, the more you become connected to what it is you're eating. When you cook a good meal from scratch from fresh ingredients and then sit down to eat it, you realize that food is not meant to be chemically preserved, prepackaged, and shipped across the world in the name of convenience. Sure, it's fine to eat out once in a while. If you cook your meals regularly, though, you'll find that it is easier to eat a healthy diet and to avoid junk food. You'll also find that staying healthy is merely a matter of choice.

Some Great and Healthy Vegetables to Cook (or Eat Raw) Include:	
Asparagus	Garlic
Beets	Herbs (parsley, basil, dill, etc.)
Bell peppers	Kale
Broccoli	Leeks
Cabbage	Onions
Carrots	Potatoes and sweet potatoes
Cauliflower	Salad greens (lettuce, arugula, tatsoi, etc.)
Collard greens	Tomatoes

And Try These Great-Tasting, Heart-Healthy Fruits and Berries:	
Apples	Oranges
Bananas	Papayas
Blackberries	Peaches
Blueberries	Pears
Kiwis	Plums
Mangoes	Raspberries
Nectarines	Strawberries

A Final Word About Eating

Ultimately, healthy eating has more to do with heeding your appetite than counting calories and scrutinizing every item that goes down the hatch. You should watch what you eat. You should avoid certain foods, especially those foods containing things like saturated fats and high cholesterol. In the end, you should listen to your hunger and think of your body as an engine requiring fuel to run. When you're hungry, eat healthy foods. Drink lots of water. And when you're full? Stop.

MYTHS and FACTS

Smoking a few cigarettes here and there won't harm you.

Smokers have more than twice the risk of heart attack as nonsmokers. The risk of heart attack, stroke, and other cardiovascular conditions increases even for those who smoke just one or two cigarettes a day. For the sake of your heart, avoid cigarettes.

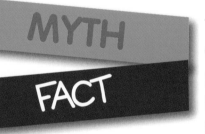

The only people who have heart disease are the ones who don't exercise and don't eat well.

Unfortunately, while lifestyle choices do often influence a person's susceptibility to heart problems, genetics and family history play a large role as well. Some people are born with weak hearts that are just more prone to breaking down.

Only males need to be concerned about preventing heart disease.

While the risk of having heart disease in one's lifetime is slightly higher in men, it is still quite high in women. In fact, it is the number one killer of women over age twenty-five in the United States. All people need to work to reduce their risk by living a heart-healthy life.

The Importance of Exercise

If there's one thing you can do right now to improve or maintain the health of your heart, it's to exercise. Stop reading, close this book, and head out the door. Run. Play. Swim, bike, join a team. The more exercise you get, the healthier you'll be.

Regular exercise is proven to be one of the easiest, most effective means of preventing heart problems. Exercise burns calories, builds muscle, and keeps your cardiovascular system in shape. Fortunately, exercising is easy. You just need to make it fun.

How Exercise Helps

Regular exercise is by far the best way to achieve overall physical fitness, which in turn is an important component of heart health.

What is physical fitness? Fitness pros say it consists of five elements: cardiorespiratory endurance, muscular strength, muscular endurance, body composition, and flexibility.

Cardiorespiratory endurance is the ability of the circulatory system (heart, blood, and blood vessels) and respiratory system (lungs and airways) to do their jobs as you exercise. The best way to improve cardiorespiratory endurance is by engaging in activities that cause your heart rate to rise for an extended period of time. The longer your pulse remains above your resting heart rate (the rate at which your heart beats

Dig deep and find the time to exercise—outdoors. The fresh air is good for your lungs, and the scenery will give you inspiration to get in shape.

when you're sitting down), the more efficient your heart becomes at doing its job. Examples of appropriate activities for improving cardio-respiratory endurance include brisk walking or running, long-distance swimming, and biking. Perhaps not surprisingly, triathletes have great cardiorespiratory endurance.

The next element of physical fitness is muscular strength. This is a measure of how effectively one's muscles can exert force during an activity. The best way to build muscular strength is by working your muscles against resistance—through weight lifting, for example.

Muscular endurance is the capacity for muscles to work continuously without getting fatigued. You can improve your muscular endurance with some of the same aerobic activities you use to improve cardiorespiratory endurance.

Another measure of physical fitness is body composition. Regular exercise results in the conversion of body fat to muscle. If you tend to carry around a few extra pounds, exercise will help you get rid of fat and improve your body composition.

Finally, flexibility is the range of motion any body part has around a joint. For example, you can measure the flexibility of your right arm by raising your arm above your head and then reaching backward. The more motion you can get out of your arm (as it rotates around the joint in your shoulder), the greater your flexibility. Forms of exercise like yoga or Pilates can improve flexibility tremendously.

Regular exercise—and the resulting improvements in one's physical fitness—has been shown to:

- Increase the body's ability to use oxygen. (Red blood cells carry more oxygen, enabling better oxygen delivery to every part of the body.)

Regular checkups with a medical professional are highly recommended. Use your visit to ask the doctor about any concerns you have.

- Lower respiratory rates during physical exertion. (Breathing during exertion becomes easier.)
- Increase blood vessel density in muscles. (More capillary blood vessels means more oxygen and better nutrition for fuel-hungry muscles.)
- Decrease coronary artery disease risk factors. (Exercise reduces blood pressure, increases good HDL cholesterol, and reduces body fat.)
- Decrease anxiety and stress and improve overall satisfaction with life.

The bottom line is when you exercise, your heart rate goes up. Your heart beats harder. In essence, your heart gets a workout, just like your legs get a workout when you run, or your arms get a workout when you swing a baseball bat or climb a rock wall. All that work, in turn, builds strength. Your heart becomes stronger, and it also becomes healthier.

First, Get a Checkup

If you are new to exercising, it is a good idea to talk to your doctor first. Schedule a checkup in which you can talk about your plans to get fit. Ask the doctor whether there are any precautions you should take based on your personal health history. Your doctor can tell you whether you should avoid certain activities and might even recommend others that you haven't considered. He or she will want to listen to your heart and do a full physical exam to make sure everything is working the way it's supposed to. Chances are, you'll get the go-ahead right away, but it's better to be safe than sorry.

If you really enjoy running, you might want to enter and train for a local race. Distances range from 5 kilometers (a little over 3 miles) to marathons.

Doctor's Recommendation: Get Up and Go

The facts are grim: nearly half of all American youths do not get exercise on a regular basis. And that lack of exercise has taken its toll. Young people today are fatter than ever—a direct result, say experts, of too little exercise combined with high-calorie diets consisting of fast, fatty, sugar-packed foods. Basically, kids are eating too much and moving too little.

And adults? Even worse. More than 50 percent of American adults don't log enough physical activity to reap the health benefits. Furthermore, a quarter of all adults do not get any exercise at all. You might not be interested in what adults do, but consider this: most of those adults who don't exercise—and who are at risk for heart problems as a result—never got into the habit while they were young. It's never too early to start exercising!

These troubling statistics may or may not apply to you. If you're already exercising, and you aren't overweight, there's likely nothing to worry about. If, on the other hand, you're a verifiable couch potato, here's the recommendation of the Centers for Disease Control and Prevention (CDC): get sixty minutes of moderate activity per day. To maximize your heart health, get more.

One hour of exercise every single day? If it sounds like too much, it shouldn't. For one, you don't have to do the entire sixty minutes all at once. If an hour straight is too hard, try ten minutes here, ten minutes there. Fit in exercise when you can. Some suggestions: Try walking (briskly) to school, playing tag, jumping rope, swimming, running, or riding a bike. Go skateboarding. Turn off your television, shut down your computer, get up, and move. Jump. Dance. Go on a hike. And whatever you do, have fun doing it.

Raise the Bar

If you're already active, here's more good news: within reason, the more exercise you get, the better. Don't overdo it, but do exercise every day.

Unless you have a heart condition that requires you to take it easy, you can set a goal to do more than one hour of exercise a day. A great way to do this is by joining a team or by signing up for an athletic event, like an organized running race, that requires you to really train to get in shape. Aim for two hours of exercise each day. However, it's fine to take a day off when you feel tired. Serious athletes alternate easy days with high-intensity days. Some take rest days when they do nothing but sit around, eat, and nap. If training sounds like something you might enjoy, go for it.

Recruit Your Friends

A great way to stay motivated and interested in exercising is to recruit your friends to join you. If, for you, exercising means playing a game outside with your neighbors, that's great. If you like to go on long bike rides or if snowboarding is your thing, it helps to have a few friends that like to do the same activities as you. Find a partner, suit up, and get out together. You might even find that you push each other to do more—to go harder or farther or faster. Even if you are just getting started, exercising with friends can make the process more enjoyable. Also, making plans with a friend to work out may help you to follow through.

You're Exercising, So Eat More

When exercise becomes a part of your daily life, you're bound to notice an increase in your appetite. When you exercise, you burn

Mountain biking is yet another fun way to get outside and exercise. Very little equipment is required: a bike, a helmet, and the nearest trail!

calories. That's why exercise, for many people, leads to weight loss. On the one hand, moderate weight loss is recommended for a lot of people who are overweight. On the other hand, if you're already thin, you probably don't want to lose more weight. Instead you'll need to compensate by eating more to balance out the calories burned by exercise. One of the great things about incorporating daily exercise into your life is the fact that eventually, weight maintenance becomes less of an issue. You'll find that it is much easier to maintain a healthy weight without worrying as much about dieting.

Heart Health Calculators

Two of the leading indicators for heart disease risk are being overweight and having high cholesterol. Fortunately, in most cases, both conditions are preventable, and both can be reliably measured.

Health professionals determine whether someone is officially overweight by calculating his or her body mass index, or BMI. BMI is a calculation involving your height and weight. At any given height, the more you weigh, the higher your BMI. A person is considered overweight if he or she has a BMI of 25 or higher. A BMI of 30 or higher is considered obese. For the CDC's Body Mass Index (BMI) Calculator, go to http://www.cdc.gov/healthyweight/assessing/bmi/index.html.

Cholesterol is measured with a blood test administered by a health professional. Most teens do not need to have their cholesterol measured. Adults, on the other hand, should have their cholesterol levels checked regularly. The CDC reports that a 10 percent decrease in blood cholesterol can reduce a person's chance of developing cardiovascular disease by up to 30 percent. It recommends that all adults have their cholesterol checked every five years. The NHLBI's National Cholesterol Education Program is a nationwide campaign to reduce illness and death from heart disease by reducing the number of people with high cholesterol. The program offers a free risk-assessment tool that estimates your chance of having a heart attack over the next ten years.

• • •

That's not to say you should follow a big workout with a trip to the local fast food joint. Eat healthy, well-rounded meals and nutritious snacks, and drink lots of water. Listen to your body, and eat when you're hungry.

Staying Safe

A last word of advice about exercise and physical fitness: safety should always come first. Some tips: When you're on the skate ramp or on the slopes, always wear a helmet. When you ride your bike, always wear a helmet. Head injuries are extremely dangerous and can be fatal.

Before you engage in high-intensity exercise (like sprints on the track or a soccer game), spend some time warming up. Jog for five to ten minutes and then stretch. Jump in place. Do push-ups and sit-ups. The last thing you want to do is to go from zero to sixty before your body is ready. If you do, you could end up with a pulled muscle, an injured tendon, or worse. Your heart will appreciate the warm-up time as well.

Chapter 4

Other Healthy Habits

There are other ways to improve heart health besides improving your diet and increasing physical activity. Reducing stress is one way. Not smoking is another. To treat your heart truly well, it takes more than one or two lifestyle changes. It takes an entirely new approach to how you live your life, how you find balance in your day-to-day activities, and how you look at yourself as a human being. Do you value your personal health? Do you want to live a long and productive life? Of course you do. Fortunately, it's not so hard to get started down that path. Focus on the areas that matter, and you'll soon see the benefits to your body, mind, and heart.

Reducing Stress

Stress has been shown to be a significant contributing factor when it comes to heart problems. Scientists have found that heart attacks in particular are commonly set off by stress. Stress also has secondary effects: sometimes people overeat when they're feeling stressed out, which can then lead to excessive weight gain. Others smoke when they're stressed.

So what causes stress? Among children and teens, stress can be caused by family problems, such as a divorce or a death of a parent or relative. School and the pressures that come with it can also be a

Too much fast food, or any kind of junk food, can lead to heart problems. Minimize fried, fast, and processed foods, and you'll be on your way to a heart-healthy life.

big source of stress. Sometimes even sports or activities can be stressful: the pressure of succeeding in a big game or competition can be very hard to handle.

Of course, stress is not going to cause you to have a heart attack now. But if you learn to deal with stress effectively as a teenager, you'll take those lessons with you into adulthood. Then, when life becomes stressful during a period when you might be more susceptible to a heart attack, you'll know how to handle it.

Reducing stress is typically a matter of dealing with the problem at hand. If your stress is caused by family trouble, it might help to talk about it with your family members. If you're not comfortable talking to them directly, you can talk to a school counselor, your doctor, or another adult whom you trust. Just getting your feelings off your chest can go a long way toward reducing stress.

Another way to reduce stress is through exercise. Some say exercise reduces stress merely by distracting the individual from the problem. Others believe there is a chemical reaction in the brain that occurs during exercise that may reduce stress. Whatever the case, try it out. A long run might be just what you need when you're feeling stressed out. Plus, there's one additional benefit: exercise, as you know, improves heart health in general.

Don't Smoke

You're probably aware by now that smoking is terrible, even deadly, for your health. It leads to breathing problems. It causes cancer. And it hurts your heart.

The CDC has determined that those who smoke are up to six times more likely than nonsmokers to have a heart attack. Those who

Heart-Healthy Tips

These tips come from the American Dietetic Association (ADA), the world's largest organization of food and nutrition professionals and a group devoted to helping people stay healthy.

1. Lose weight if you're overweight. Shedding the extra pounds will make it easier for your heart to do its job.
2. Cut back on fats. Avoid trans fat, saturated fat, and cholesterol by choosing foods that are healthy: lean meats like chicken and fish and low-fat cheese, yogurt, and milk.
3. Reduce sodium by eating foods with no added salt and by not adding salt to foods you prepare yourself. When buying canned goods, pay close attention to the label for reduced-salt or no-salt choices.
4. Eat lots of fruits and vegetables, which contain heart-healthy fiber, vitamins, and minerals. In general, the more colorful the fruit or vegetable, the better. Go to a farmer's market to see what's available in your area. Chances are, you'll find all kinds of options you've never considered before.
5. Eat plenty of whole grains, including whole-grain cereals, whole-wheat bread, whole-wheat pasta, and brown rice. The ADA recommends at least three ounces of whole-grain foods daily, but the more, the better.
6. Eat fish. Fish like salmon, trout, and herring are rich in healthy omega-3 fatty acids.
7. Eat foods with unsaturated fats like vegetable oils, nuts, and seeds.
8. Get lots of fiber. You can find it in foods like oatmeal, barley, fruits, vegetables, and beans.
9. Read labels for calories, fat, cholesterol, sodium, and nutrient content. Every packaged item has a label. Make it a habit to check it out!
10. Exercise! Try to get thirty minutes or more a day, even if you have to do it in ten-minute intervals.

smoke more are also more likely to have heart problems. Smoking also increases risk for stroke. Secondhand smoke can be just as deadly as smoking cigarettes yourself. Nonsmokers who are regularly exposed to secondhand smoke are 60 percent more likely to develop heart disease than those who are not.

Again, if you're smoking now, you probably won't have a heart attack tomorrow. But you are significantly increasing the risk that you will when you're an adult. In addition, the earlier people start smoking, the more likely they are to become addicted. If you start smoking now, you're putting yourself in serious danger.

Get Plenty of Sleep

Another important component of heart health—and, for that matter, health in general—is adequate sleep. Children and teens especially need lots of sleep because of the demands placed on their bodies (and minds) by growth and development.

With every inch you grow and every pound you gain, you're also building your heart. And just as you need to eat a healthy diet to fuel that growth, you need to sleep to allow your growing body to rest. In fact, a good portion of the growth we all go through occurs during sleep.

According to the National Sleep Foundation (NSF), school-aged children ages five through twelve need ten to eleven hours of sleep per night in order to be fully rested. The average schoolkid, however, gets just 9.5 hours of sleep. And almost 70 percent of children regularly experience sleeping problems.

Experts blame sleeping problems on a variety of factors, but the two biggest are caffeine consumption and televisions in bedrooms. If you drink beverages that contain caffeine, you can expect to lose an average of 3.5 hours of sleep per week. If you have a television in

When your schedule is packed to the hilt, adequate sleep gives your growing body time to catch up.

your bedroom, you stand to lose about two hours of sleep per week to watching your favorite programs.

And then there's the problem of getting up for school. Thanks to the body's normal sleep-wake rhythms, most children, and especially teenagers, aren't physiologically ready to fall asleep early enough to squeeze in nine-plus hours before it's time to get up for those early school days.

It all adds up to what sleep experts call sleep debt: the hours of sleep the body owes itself but can never seem to afford thanks to things like television, school, sports, and other factors. If you've ever found yourself yawning uncontrollably in the middle of the day (or have even accidentally fallen asleep in school), you know what sleep deprivation is.

Some solutions? First, don't drink soda or other high-sugar, high-caffeine beverages. If you have to watch TV or use the computer, call it quits after dinner and definitely keep these forms of entertainment out of your bedroom. Try to eat dinner relatively early—say at six o'clock. Try napping on the weekends to catch up and reduce your sleep debt. Make your bedroom conducive to sleeping—that is, dark, cool, and quiet. And finally, consider reading. There's nothing like a good book to relax you and even signal to the brain that it's time to go to sleep.

Try New Activities

We spent an entire chapter learning about the value of exercise. Here are a few more body-friendly activities that fall outside the realm of what most would consider exercise:

Wii: Chances are, you've heard of Nintendo's latest offering. The Nintendo Wii gaming system simulates the moves you'd make if you

Yoga and meditation are good for the body, mind, and heart. If you've never tried yoga, sign up for a class at school or at a local studio.

were playing real sports, only it lets you do so inside in the comfort of your own home. If it's raining, for example, or you have a medical condition that doesn't allow you to get outside, you can fire up your Wii and play tennis, golf, or baseball. You probably won't work up the kind of sweat you would doing the real thing. You will move, though, and some swear it's a great way to get in shape. Try it out.

Yoga, tai chi, etc.: Some say these practices are relaxing and meditative. Others feel they work their muscles like nothing else. Still others find they're a bit of both. Whatever the case, "alternative" activities based on ancient Eastern traditions like yoga, tai chi, and the martial arts are great for the mind, body, and spirit.

Get a dog: If your parents will go for it, consider getting a dog. If there's one thing on which dog owners can agree, it's that raising a puppy and caring for a dog requires a huge amount of energy. If you'd like to increase your physical activity, get a dog and be the one in your family who takes it on regular walks and runs.

Try a new hobby: Learn to paint. Play an instrument. Take up ballet or gymnastics. When you take up an activity that truly interests you, it's easier to find the energy it takes to stay healthy. Devote yourself to a hobby, and you may be less likely to treat your body poorly by eating out of boredom and watching too much television. Plus, wouldn't it benefit you to have a strong set of lungs if you'll be playing the trumpet in your school band? And what could be more stress relieving than painting a mural or sketching passersby in a local park?

General Life Balance

There's a message that links everything you've read so far concerning heart health: to maximize heart health, you need to maximize your

Begin heart-healthy habits today, and you will be more likely to enjoy a long and active life.

general health. The heart is such an important part of your body that you can't be healthy if your heart isn't healthy. And you can't have a healthy heart if your body is neglected and falling apart.

The healthiest people are those who make healthy choices throughout their lives, from their teenage years to old age. Health for a lifetime does not come automatically to many people. It takes work. If you start now when you're young, you're far more likely to develop the habits you'll need to carry you through life. You may not have heart problems now, and you may never have them if you're lucky. But you can significantly reduce your risk for heart problems in the future by living a heart-healthy life today.

Talk to the healthiest people you know, and they'll probably tell you this: healthy living is not so difficult, and it's enjoyable. Yes, it involves making wise choices, but those choices are easy to make when your health is a priority. Healthy habits come easily when they're fun (like playing on a soccer team), tasty (like eating your favorite heart-healthy meal), stress reducing (like taking ten minutes every day to sit in silence), or when they just feel good. Remember, your heart is a very important organ in your body. Every single time it beats, it's a sign that you're alive. Help it beat its best, and you'll help yourself to thrive.

artery Any of the branching blood vessels that carry oxygen-rich blood away from the heart to the body's cells, tissues, and organs.

atherosclerosis The narrowing and hardening of the arteries due to a buildup of plaque on the artery walls. Over time, blood flow to the organs can become restricted, leading to heart attack, stroke, or even death.

atrium One of the two upper chambers of the heart. It receives blood from the veins and forces it into a ventricle.

blood pressure A measure of the force exerted by the movement of blood on blood vessel walls.

body mass index (BMI) The measure of height versus weight to determine whether an individual is within a healthy weight range for his or her height.

calorie A unit used to express the heat-producing or energy-producing value of food.

cancer A sometimes deadly condition involving the uncontrolled growth of abnormal cells.

cardiorespiratory Relating to the heart and the respiratory system.

cardiovascular Pertaining to the heart and the blood vessels of the body.

cholesterol A substance found in the body and necessary for life but that can be harmful at abnormally high levels in the bloodstream.

congenital Present at birth.

coronary Of or relating to the heart, or the coronary arteries and veins of the heart.

genetics The genetic makeup—the inherited genes—of an organism.

heart attack A sudden interruption of the normal functioning of the heart often caused by an obstruction in an artery that supplies the heart with blood.

obese Severely overweight.

organ A distinctive body part with a specific function.

plaque Deposits of fat, cholesterol, calcium, and other substances found on some inner artery walls.

risk factor A habit, condition, or circumstance that increases the chance an individual will have a particular health problem.

secondhand smoke Smoke that travels to and is inhaled by a nonsmoker.

stress Physical, mental, or emotional strain and tension, capable of affecting one's physical health.

stroke A medical condition occurring when the blood supply to the brain is partially or completely obstructed by a blood clot.

vein Any of the branching blood vessels that carry blood toward the heart.

ventricle One of the two lower chambers of the heart. It receives blood from an atrium and pumps it into the arteries.

American Heart Association (AHA)

7272 Greenville Avenue

Dallas, TX 75231

(800) 242-8721

Web site: http://www.americanheart.org

The AHA's mission is to reduce deaths resulting from cardiovascular disease and stroke. Promoting fitness is just one way the AHA achieves that goal.

Centers for Disease Control and Prevention

1600 Clifton Road

Atlanta, Georgia 30333

(800) CDC-INFO (232-4636)

Web site: http://www.cdc.gov

The CDC, a part of the U.S. Department of Health and Human Services, is a great source of credible information on all aspects of health and fitness.

Health Canada

Address Locator 0900C2

Ottawa, ON K1A 0K9

Canada

(866) 225-0709

Web site: http://www.hc-sc.gc.ca

Canada's federal agency responsible for helping citizens maintain and improve their health, Health Canada provides all the information you'll need to get active and make healthy choices a part of your life.

National Heart, Lung, and Blood Institute (NHLBI)
Health Information Center
P.O. Box 30105
Bethesda, MD 20824-0105
(301) 592-8573
Heart Health Information Line: (800) 575-WELL (9355)
Web site: http://www.nhlbi.nih.gov
The NHLBI provides information on heart disease, its prevention, and its treatment.

National Institutes of Health
9000 Rockville Pike
Bethesda, MD 20892
(301) 496-4000
Web site: http://www.nih.gov
The NIH is a division of the U.S. Department of Health and Human Services. It conducts and supports medical research and, like the CDC, is an excellent source of health information.

Web Sites

Due to the changing nature of Internet links, Rosen Publishing has developed an online list of Web sites related to the subject of this book. This site is updated regularly. Please use this link to access the list:

http://www.rosenlinks.com/hab/heart

American Medical Association. *American Medical Association Family Medical Guide*. Hoboken, NJ: John Wiley & Sons, 2004.

Ballard, Carol. *Keeping Fit: Body Systems*. Chicago, IL: Heinemann Library, 2008.

Corbin, Charles B., Guy C. Le Masurier, and Dolly Lambdin. *Fitness for Life: Middle School*. Champaign, IL: Human Kinetics, 2007.

Doeden, Matt. *Eat Right! How You Can Make Good Food Choices*. Minneapolis, MN: Lerner Publications Company, 2009.

Doeden, Matt. *Stay Fit! How You Can Get in Shape*. Minneapolis, MN: Lerner Publications Company, 2009.

Gray, Susan Heinrichs. *The Heart*. Chanhassen, MN: Child's World, 2006.

Green, Jen. *Blood and Heart*. Mankato, MN: Stargazer Books, 2006.

Haney, Johannah. *Heart Disease*. New York, NY: Benchmark Books, 2005.

Libal, Autumn. *The Importance of Physical Activity and Exercise: The Fitness Factor* (Obesity). Philadelphia, PA: Mason Crest Publishers, 2006.

McCarthy, Rose. *Food Labels: Using Nutrition Information to Create a Healthy Diet* (Library of Nutrition). New York, NY: Rosen Publishing Group, 2005.

Piscatella, Joseph C., and Barry A. Franklin. *Take a Load Off Your Heart: 109 Things You Can Actually Do to Prevent, Halt, and Reverse Heart Disease*. New York, NY: Workman Publishing Company, Inc., 2003.

Silverstein, Alvin, Virginia B. Silverstein, and Laura Silverstein Nunn. *Heart Disease*. Minneapolis, MN: Twenty-First Century Books, 2006.

BIBLIOGRAPHY

American College of Sports Medicine. *ACSM's Guidelines for Exercise Testing and Prescription*. 6th ed. Baltimore, MD: Lippincott Williams & Wilkins, 2000.

American Dietetic Association. "Tips for a Healthy Heart." Eatright.org. Retrieved August 22, 2009 (www.eatright.org/cps/rde/xchg/ada/hs.xsl/nutrition_19748_ENU_HTML.htm).

American Heart Association. "How to Make Fast Food Friendlier." Retrieved September 3, 2009 (www.americanheart.org/presenter.jhtml?identifier=3033900).

Boron, Walter F., and Emile L. Boulpaep. *Medical Physiology: A Cellular and Molecular Approach*. Philadelphia, PA: Elsevier Science, 2003.

Centers for Disease Control and Prevention. "Heart Disease." Retrieved August 21, 2009 (www.cdc.gov/HeartDisease/index.htm).

Centers for Disease Control and Prevention. "Physical Activity for Everyone." Retrieved August 17, 2009 (www.cdc.gov/physicalactivity/everyone/guidelines/children.html).

EurekAlert. "Eating Out Often May Add to Kids' Cardiovascular Risk." November 14, 2005. Retrieved September 3, 2009 (www.eurekalert.org/pub_releases/2005-11/aha-eoo110705.php).

National Heart, Lung, and Blood Institute. "High Blood Cholesterol: What You Need to Know." Retrieved August 21, 2009 (http://www.nhlbi.nih.gov/health/public/heart/chol/wyntk.htm).

National Heart, Lung, and Blood Institute. "Questions to Ask Your Doctor, HHS, NIH, NHLBI." Retrieved August 25, 2009 (http://www.nhlbi.nih.gov/educational/hearttruth/lower-risk/ask-doctor.htm).

National Sleep Foundation. "Children and Sleep." Retrieved September 12, 2009 (www.sleepfoundation.org/article/sleep-topics/children-and-sleep).

Sandmaier, Marian. "Your Guide to a Healthy Heart." U.S. Department of Health and Human Services, National Institutes of Health, National Heart, Lung, and Blood Institute. NIH Publication No. 06-5269, 2005.

Texas Heart Institute. "Heart Disease Risk Factors for Children and Teenagers." Retrieved August 18, 2009 (www.texasheartinstitute.org/hic/topics/hsmart/children_risk_factors.cfm).

INDEX

About the Author

Michael R. Wilson is a health and science writer. He's written about many topics for Rosen Publishing, including the human brain, the cardiopulmonary system, and genetics.

Photo Credits